HR BY
Design

Solving HR Challenges
with Design Thinking

Jodi Brandstetter

Influence Network Media

Contents

Introduction

In my senior year in high school, I had my life figured out. I was going to be an FBI Profiler like Jodie Foster in *Silence of the Lambs*. In college, I would go on to study Criminology and Psychology and eventually make my way to Quantico. One of my favorite teachers, Mr. Blackwell, sat me down and had a heart-to-heart with me about my future plans. He helped me realize that getting into the FBI may be harder than I thought and maybe I should study something else. His suggestion was Finance. Now Mr. Blackwell wasn't just a teacher, he was my middle school gym teacher, Assistant Principal in high school, and my driver's education teacher. The life of a small-town girl! He had been in my life for 7 years and I truly respected him and his opinion.

So what did I do?

I went to the University of Evansville and majored in Finance. And I hated it!

The major was not a success but going into business was definitely my future. I just needed to find the right spot. Luckily, I listened to everyone's advice and got an internship at a local hospital in Human Resources (HR). I figured I could look at job descriptions and be inspired. What actually inspired me was HR. I loved the interaction with people and helping them in all areas of Human Resources from benefits to finding a job. I immediately changed my major to Management.

And 20+ years later, I am still loving everything about HR.

My focus has been on Talent Acquisition and a few years ago I learned about design thinking and fell in love with it. It is the creative problem-solving method for solving hiring challenges. And it works with HR challenges too. My first book, *Hire By Design*, provided different ways you can use design thinking in talent acquisition.

Now I want to show how you can use design thinking in Human Resources. This book serves as a guidebook for HR professionals who are tired of the same old solutions and want to get creative with solving HR Challenges. I hope this inspires you to get out of your box and create amazing solutions for your company.

~Jodi Brandstetter, Design Thinker and Lover of HR

I.

HR and Design Thinking

As a long-term Human Resource (HR) professional who believes in our industry, I decided to google, "Human Resources is" and this is what came up:

Google

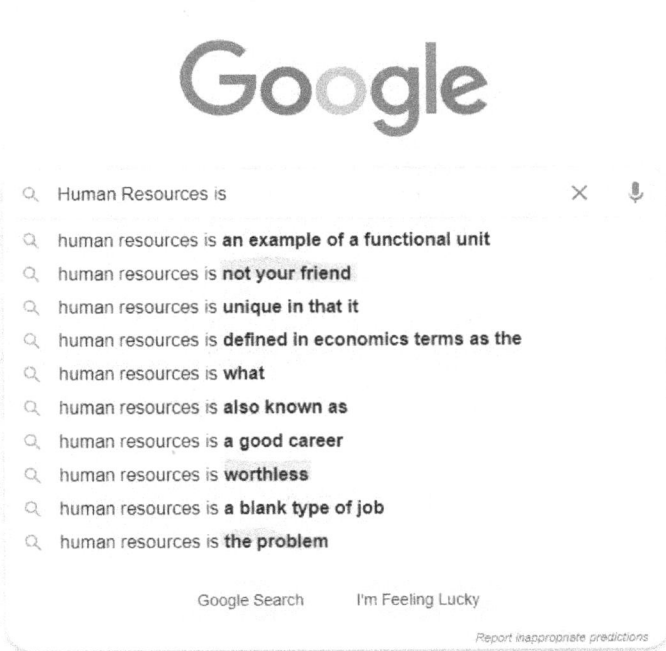

| Q | Human Resources is | × | 🎤 |

Q human resources is **an example of a functional unit**
Q human resources is **not your friend**
Q human resources is **unique in that it**
Q human resources is **defined in economics terms as the**
Q human resources is **what**
Q human resources is **also known as**
Q human resources is **a good career**
Q human resources is **worthless**
Q human resources is **a blank type of job**
Q human resources is **the problem**

Google Search   I'm Feeling Lucky

Report inappropriate predictions

The highlighted items are the ones are in question here. "HR is not your friend." "HR is worthless." "HR is the problem."

Definitely not what the HR industry wants to see when googled.

Now there are some good ones here too. "HR is an example of a functional unit." "HR is a good career." My personal favorite is "HR is a blank type of job." Wonder what the blank stands for!

There are a lot of stereotypes that HR has about people outside of it. And HR is more than the "no to everything" or "party police" or "fire and cut the employee's badge" people. HR's goal is to ensure a business has the people operations to fulfill the business goals and objectives. People operations can be HR strategies including culture, organizational design, employee engagement, total compensation, talent acquisition and management, performance management, and learning and development.

People are vital for success in a business. Depending on the type and size of a business, 40% to 80% of gross revenue is spent on employee salaries and benefits combined. [1] That is a lot of the budget that is dedicated to people. People operations is a very important aspect to the success of a business.

Why Use Design Thinking Methodology in HR?

HR and People Operations is challenging. There are a lot of factors that go into ensuring employees have everything they need to be successful in their role and ensure it fits within the company budget. And there is also ensuring that the company meets its goals and objectives to consider. Having a way to solve problems in a creative way that focuses on the business and people is vital for success in Human Resources. And that is exactly what design thinking can do.

In order to solve a problem for people, one must be able to understand the people and ensure the solution works for those people. Design thinking does this! And to come up with creative and "outside the box" ideas, brainstorming needs to happen. Design thinking does this! If HR is going to update a process or add new benefits and update technology, they need to test drive before finalizing. In my old job, this was known as "putting it in the sandbox." And, yes, design thinking does this.

Design thinking is the methodology for Human Resources. It combines everything HR needs to create solutions that work for both the business and its people.

In this book, I am going to provide a deep dive into design thinking and utilize design thinking to provide a solution to an HR challenge. By the end of the book, design thinking will be a no-brainer for any HR professional to use in their role. Also, I am going to provide some HR stories from some amazing HR professionals that highlight how HR can change its perspective on employees, management, and leaders of businesses.

Before diving into solving an HR challenge, understanding design thinking is needed.

Notes

1. https://smallbusiness.chron.com/percent-business-budget-salary-14254.html

2.

Understanding Design Thinking

Designing thinking is commonly referred to as "creating products, technology, and apps." It can be used in all areas of business including HR. Tim Brown, Executive Chair of IDEO, a global design company, defines design thinking as:

> "Design thinking is a human-centered approach to innovation that draws from the designer's toolkit to integrate the needs of people, the possibilities of technology, and the requirements for business success,[1]"

Design thinking looks at a problem or challenge and ensures that it is desirable for the audience, viable for the business, and feasible to accomplish. When using design thinking, you need to always be thinking about desirability, viability, and feasibility to ensure the solution meets both the person and the business.

Here is the framework for design thinking methodology:

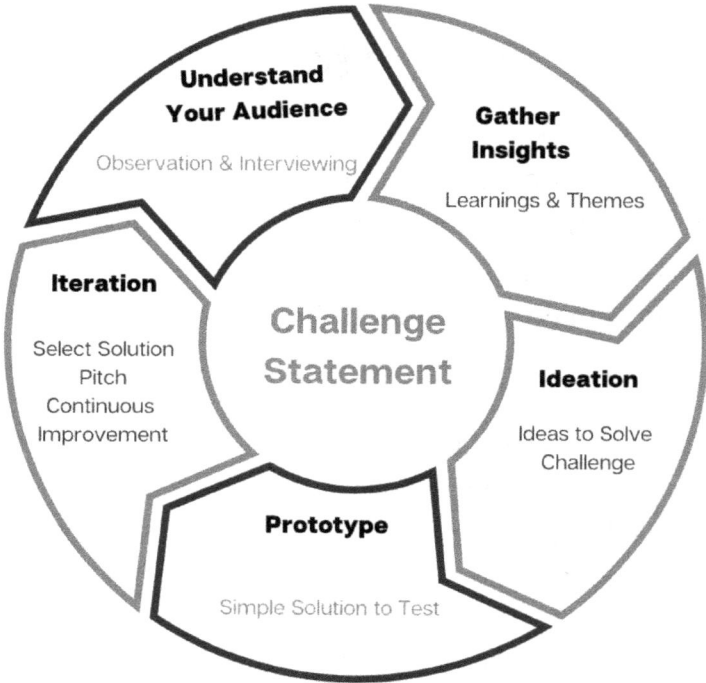

Challenge Statement

The first step in the design thinking process is having a question that needs answering. Typically, the question starts like this: "How might we ...?" The question focuses on the following:

- The What: what is the problem or challenge?
- The Audience: who is the audience or key stakeholders?
- The Change: what is the change you want to see and what is the timeline?
- Inspiring and Interesting: are you, or the team, excited and interested in solving the challenge?

Once the Challenge Statement is created, you need to review it and ensure that it is focused on the need, broad enough to make discoveries, and manageable. Using the imagery of *Goldilocks and the Three Bears*, three types of questions emerge: is it too broad and unmanageable, too narrow and limits the possible solutions, or is it Goldilocks's "just right" which is focused on need, broad enough to make discoveries, and manageable.

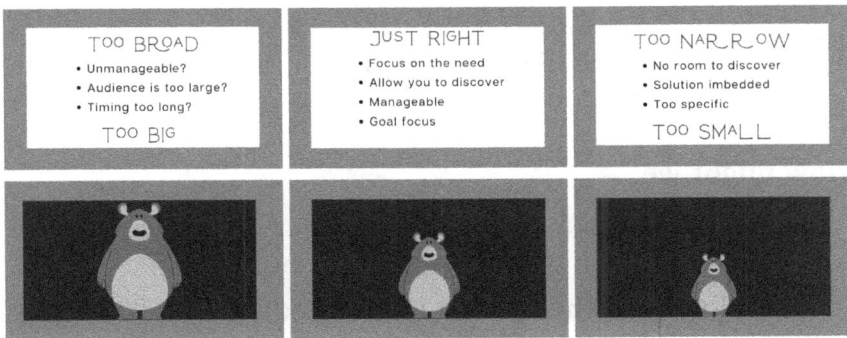

TOO BROAD	JUST RIGHT	TOO NARROW
• Unmanageable? • Audience is too large? • Timing too long? TOO BIG	• Focus on the need • Allow you to discover • Manageable • Goal focus	• No room to discover • Solution imbedded • Too specific TOO SMALL

Now that the challenge statement is just right, there are a few more questions to ask to ensure the Challenge Statement will work.

1. Is the solution in the statement?

- Yes? Go back and update the challenge statement so that there is no solution included. This limits your creativity.

2. Are you excited about learning more?

   - No? Go back to update the challenge statement so that it is interesting for the team who is working on the challenge.

3. Is it focused on your audience and on a specific timeframe

   - No? Add audience and timeframe into the statement.

Here are a few examples:

How might we...

- Create a working environment for our hybrid employees in the US that inspires collaboration during the first 90 days?
- Encourage our middle management to learn more about unconscious bias and take these learnings to their teams this year?
- Create an onboarding experience for our new hires that will inspire loyalty and dedication to our core

values and ensure that the hires are inspired to create their best work?

The Challenge Statement sets the tone of the design thinking process. And the next step sets the tone on who the solution will be focused on.

Understand Your Audience

In order to create a solution, understanding the audience is key. The solution has to meet the audience's expectations. How horrible would it be if the solution in the end failed? Just think about all that time, energy, and money wasted. All because due diligence did not happen upfront.

When understanding the audience, is a three-step process. The first step is Immersion in Empathy, the second step is Observation, and the third is Interviewing. But before you start on these, there is a question that needs to be answered first. Who is the audience?

Audience Persona

There is a way to understand who should be observed and interviewed. It is known as the Audience Persona. The

Audience Persona gives the ability to understand the audience's values, motivators, and experiences. The Persona can also help find and engage the audience.

Here are some examples of motivators, behaviors & traits, experience, and values. As well as how to engage.

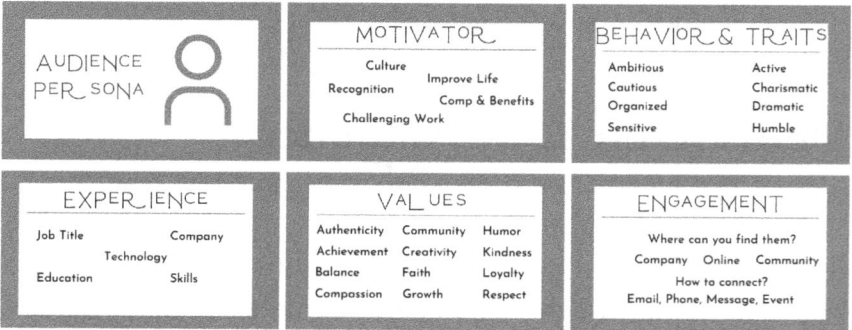

AUDIENCE PERSONA	MOTIVATOR	BEHAVIOR & TRAITS
	Culture	Ambitious / Active
	Recognition / Improve Life	Cautious / Charismatic
	Comp & Benefits	Organized / Dramatic
	Challenging Work	Sensitive / Humble
EXPERIENCE	**VALUES**	**ENGAGEMENT**
Job Title / Company	Authenticity / Community / Humor	Where can you find them?
Technology	Achievement / Creativity / Kindness	Company / Online / Community
Education / Skills	Balance / Faith / Loyalty	How to connect?
	Compassion / Growth / Respect	Email, Phone, Message, Event

Once you have the Audience Persona completed, you can focus on understanding the audience with empathy, observation, and interviewing.

Immersion in Empathy

Empathy is vital in design thinking. Understanding your target audience's perspective helps you create a solution that works for them. Observation is a great way to use empathy but there are times that observation cannot happen. This is when you are able to immerse yourself into empathy to understand the audience.

Per IDEOU, the design thinking online learning arm of IDEO, there are four ways to immerse in empathy[2]:

- Change Your Perspective – think of ways to change your perspective to relate to someone who sees things differently.
- Limit Yourself – take an ability away and explore that experience.
- Do It Yourself – try out the product, service, or experience firsthand.
- Engage in an Analogous Experience – experience, yourself, what you are designing analogously.

Think about the audience and come up with different ways to understand their perspective. The question will start with, "What does it feel like to...?" Once you complete one of the immersions in empathy, reflect on the experience and note any insights from the experience. Immersion in Empathy will also help you with questions for the interview step.

Observation

Observation is all about using eyes and ears. It is like being a fly on the wall and soaking up as much information about the audience as you can. Seeing the audience in their environment and being able to understand how they do what they do, helps to ensure any ideas or solutions can work for them.

When observing, you have to be prepared. Preparation includes deciding what individuals to observe, where to observe, and what you are looking for in your observation. Creating a game plan for observation will help to ensure that it is a success.

When observing, there are key items to be focused on. First, come with an open mind and do not be judgmental. Use your ears and eyes while observing. Focus on the what, how, and why.

- What are they doing?
- How are they doing it?
- Why are they doing it?
- Are there any behaviors, adaptations, patterns, or anything unexpected that they are doing to create an easier process?

Write notes based on the observation and jot down any questions to ask during the interview step.

If you are unsure if observation can happen with your target audience, you can also use Immersion in Empathy.

Interviewing

This comes after observation and/or immersion in empathy. You should have questions that you want to ask your audience. This is the time to ask those questions. Just like with observation, preparation is key. You will want to select the individuals you want to interview. This can be individuals you observed or different individuals. Just make sure that they meet your audience persona. And create around ten questions to ask. These questions can help with understanding the person better, understanding the challenge more clearly, and coming up with a solution.

During the interview, you want to paint the picture of the interview. I typically will thank them for helping me and let them know that this conversation will take approximately 30 to 45 minutes. I also let them know that I will be taking notes or recording the interview to help me retain the conversation.

While conducting the interview, good eye contact and body language conveying your interest is key. This can look like leaning forward or nodding. This helps the interviewee feel confident in the conversation and in themselves.

Take notes based on what you see and hear. Jot down any stories that were of interest and any insights from the interviewee. The information from observation and interviews will guide the ideation step.

Gathering Insights

Taking the time to review all of your notes from the observation and interviews will guide the next step of ideation. Review the notes and organize them into themes. This will help decide on what you want to focus on with finding the solution. It also helps you provide an update on the challenge with key stakeholders. You can update through a presentation, storyboard, or just by telling a story.

Ideation

My favorite step of design thinking is ideation. This is where creativity and innovation happen. Ideation is the step where you take time to come up with different ideas to solve the challenge. The most common ideation practice is brainstorming. There are different ways to brainstorm including brainstorming alone, in a group, mash-up, and e-storm.

To brainstorm, grab a timer, some paper or post-its, and a pen. If doing this alone, decide on the amount of time you're going to give yourself for brainstorming, and write down all your ideas during that time. With a group, you will use the same concept but take time at the end to listen to everyone's ideas and, as a group, vote and agree upon the idea to move forward with. Mash-up is completing two brainstorms with different topics and then mash those ideas together for a solution. E-storm gives you the ability to ask people from all around the world to help with ideas by emailing them the challenge question.

The main goal with ideation is to be open and think of as many ideas as possible. Let your imagination go wild. Then you take those ideas and bucket them into themes and select the idea you want to move forward with to prototype.

Prototype

Now it is time to create the prototype of the potential solution. This needs to be simple, easy, and inexpensive. A prototype is *not* the solution. It is a *possible* solution that needs to be reviewed and confirmed that it will work for the people and the business.

Prototypes can be simple and created with duct tape and cardboard. They also can be a spreadsheet, document, pilot, or storyboard.

Here are some examples of prototypes:

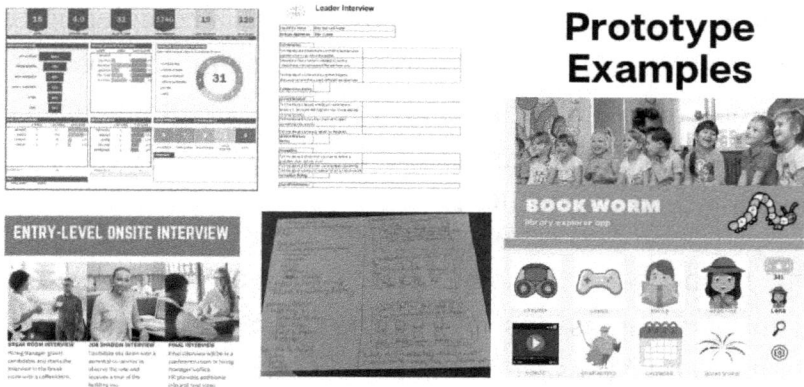

Prototype Examples

ENTRY-LEVEL ONSITE INTERVIEW

BOOK WORM

Gathering feedback from the key stakeholders and the targeted audience will help make the prototype into a solution. It may just need a few tweaks or may have to start all over. Once the prototype is the solution, pitching the solution and implementing it is next.

Iteration

I always say nothing in life or business is constant; except for change. Iteration is continuing to improve the solution. Once a solution is pitched and ready to go, implementing the solution is part of the iteration step. While implementing and using the solution, updates and enhancements can be created. Keep open communication with the target audience and the business to ensure the solution is still working, and be willing to go through the design thinking process again if needed.

The design thinking process is not perfect; just like humans are not perfect. But it does provide a tool where creativity and innovation happen. Moving forward in this book, I will use the design thinking process to create a solution within the HR space. This will provide you with the ability to see design thinking in action and give you confidence in using design thinking in your day-to-day life.

Notes

1. https://designthinking.ideo.com/
2. https://ideou.com

3.

Challenge Statement

My life has been centered around accomplishments. As a child, I was always focused on getting all A's and being on winning the sports team. And as an adult, my focus has been on climbing the corporate ladder and, now, being a successful entrepreneur. Expectations like these are not great for your mental health. I have always been an anxious person, and my inner self-talk has always been my bully. I would say that I had pre-existing conditions of burnout.

In 2015, I was working in corporate as a Talent Acquisition Director. I had six direct reports and was responsible for hiring in multiple locations. It was a demanding job that I loved and was really good at. At this point in my life, work was my baby and I was 100% dedicated to my job. And just like that life happens and I give birth to my beautiful daughter, Lena. She came 5 weeks early just to mess with my plans of preparing for maternity leave and gave me the best St. Patrick's Day gift ever. During my maternity leave, I was able to focus on her and my family and it was really nice to be dedicated to them during this time. But I was also itching to get back to work. I may have reviewed my email and taken a few meetings during maternity leave. Like I said before, I was accomplishment-centric!

Once I was back to work after my maternity leave, I was ready to give 100% to work, my daughter, my husband, *and* myself. Now I might not be the best in math but I do know you cannot give 400% to *anything*. I tried to do this for around 8 months before I had a full-on meltdown. My meltdown included high anxiety and panic attacks. It was too much for me, my body, and my brain. I was exhausted and frustrated that I was not giving my all to everyone and everything. In short: I was burnt out.

Coming back to work as a mom, made me realize that the expectations that I had for myself, as well as my company, did not change after this huge life change of becoming a mother. I realized that I could not give my 100% at work, and my work only knew me as the 100% that I had provided over the past six years. If I was going to give myself the space to focus on family *and* my work, I could not stay in that role. So, I decided to quit my job in 2018 and started my own consulting business. Now, this did not completely solve my problem of *not* giving my all, but it did give me some space to work on myself and provide myself grace and realign my priorities in life and work.

In 2018, a Gallup Survey of nearly 7,500 full-time employees found that 23% reported feeling burnt out. And that was 2018; a pre-Covid world. I'm sure that this number has only skyrocketed since 2018. Burnout can cause lots of issues at a company. Sales can go down. The best employees quit. And engagement can decrease. And who is supposed to solve these problems? Human Resources of course! But what if

HR is also burnt out? With the pandemic, government regulations, the skill gap, and the future of work, HR professionals are also similarly burnt out.

There are a lot of expectations on human resources to foster a healthy work environment for employees. And yet they are employees too; so what about them? How can HR help foster a healthy work environment if their work environment is not healthy?

I've decided for my challenge for this book, I am going to focus on HR Burnout and how to help HR with this *while* helping employees with the same.

The first step is to decide on my challenge statement. It is a process to finalize your challenge statement. Here is the process I completed.

Identify the problem/challenge:

Burnout is a concern for companies; HR typically handles this type of problem but they are also burnout. How can burnt-out employees help other employees with burnout? HR needs a solution on helping them with burnout before they can help their employees.

What do you know about this already?

I know that burnout can be based on workload, work/family needs, and support system(s). I also know that HR typically focuses on others and not themselves when it comes to wellness. There are tools and services available to assist with burnout.

Why do you want to change this?

Burnout can hurt someone in many ways. Being able to have tools or ways to cope can help with this. And emotional/mental wellness is just as important as physical wellness. Having an impact on others' wellness would be worthwhile.

How Might We Statement:

How might we provide a tool or service to help HR professionals with burnout while they help employees with their burnout?

Review Challenge Statement and ask:

Is the solution in the statement? No.

Are you excited or interested in learning more? A little.

Is it focus on your audience and focus on a specific timeframe? No.

Final Challenge Statement:

How might we take the burnout question, and focus on finding a solution for the HR team that can be implemented for other departments in the company?

With the challenge statement, the next step is to Understand the Audience with empathy, observation, and interviewing.

Challenge Statement Template:

"How Might We..." Statements needs to include:

The What – what is the problem or challenge?

The Audience – who is the audience or key stakeholders

The Change – what is the change you want to see?

Inspiring and Interesting – is the team interested/excited?

Identify the problem/challenge:

What do you know about this already?

Why do you want to change this?

How might We Statement:

Review Challenge Statement:

Is the solution in statement? Are you excited in learning more? Is it focused on your audience & a timeframe?

Final Statement:

4.

Understand Your Audience

When the SHRM conference is in Las Vegas, you may not make it to the actual conference. And a lot of times the Vegas saying, "What Happens in Vegas, Stays in Vegas" is a true statement! While chatting with my amazing friend and an amazing HR professional, Kate Legters, she explained how a session at SHRM19 helped her evaluate her company's bereavement policy. The session was *Employee Trauma: What Happened in Vegas Didn't Stay in Vegas* and in that session the speaker, Lisa D. Murfield, SHRM-SCP, provided ways to show compassion to employees and how to craft HR policies to provide that compassion [1].

Kate brought that session home with her and decided to review her company's current bereavement policy. She realized that the policy really did not demonstrate the compassion that her company wished to provide to its employees. She decided to update the bereavement policy with an open allotment of time for employees and include miscarriages and pets on the list of potential reasons to use bereavement.

Kate understood the company's focus on its employees as well as the employees at her company to establish an HR policy that works for them. This is a great example of understanding your audience.[2]

Understanding your audience gives you the ability to use and lead with empathy when solving the challenge. Putting yourself into someone else's shoes and really getting to understand them. With design thinking, you can use immersion in empathy, observation, and interviewing. Once you understand your audience, you can take your findings and insights and look for themes to help with moving forward to ideation.

For my challenge, I need to understand the following audience:

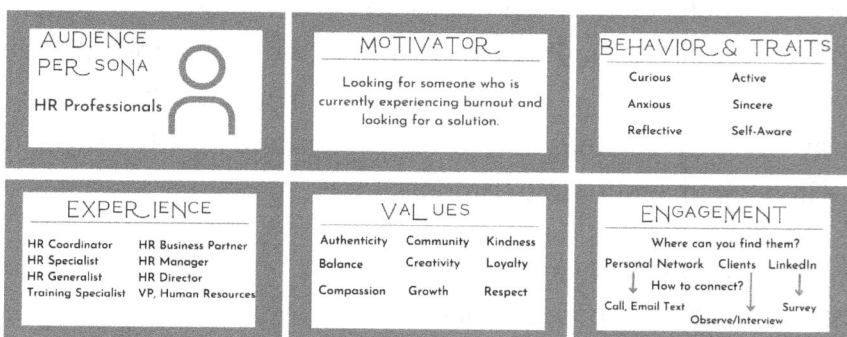

AUDIENCE PERSONA	MOTIVATOR	BEHAVIOR & TRAITS		
HR Professionals	Looking for someone who is currently experiencing burnout and looking for a solution.	Curious / Anxious / Reflective		Active / Sincere / Self-Aware

EXPERIENCE		VALUES			ENGAGEMENT
HR Coordinator / HR Specialist / HR Generalist / Training Specialist	HR Business Partner / HR Manager / HR Director / VP, Human Resources	Authenticity / Balance / Compassion	Community / Creativity / Growth	Kindness / Loyalty / Respect	Where can you find them? Personal Network / Clients / LinkedIn — How to connect? Call, Email Text / Survey / Observe/Interview

Audience Persona:

After completing my Audience Persona, I realized that I had a lot of options as to who I can reach out to for this challenge. With my 20+ years in Talent Acquisition, I have been able to connect with a lot of HR professionals. I can think of a solid six HR professionals who I consider my mentors, the best of the best in HR, and my friends. Also, in my consulting business, I work with HR professionals on a daily basis. There are a lot of opportunities to observe my clients for this challenge. And I love LinkedIn surveys. I use them all the time; so this gives me another reason to use the survey option!

Before I leap into Understanding My Audience, I need a plan. I need to know how I will immerse myself in empathy, who, where, and what I am observing; who I will interview and what will I ask in that interview. By having a plan, you will get the most out of your time and ensure that you are getting everything you need to help find a solution for your target audience.

Immersion in Empathy

Questions for Immersion in Empathy:

What does it feel like to be working in burnout?

What does it feel like to be ensuring others are not experiencing burnout while experiencing burnout yourself?

Game Plan:

Engage in an Analogous Experience: utilize LinkedIn

Surveys and ask HR professionals through a post to gain others' perspectives, and ask probing questions based on those findings.

Jodi Brandstetter
Best Selling Author CEO & Entrepreneur Speaker Self-Publishing C...
1w · Edited · 🌐

#HumanResources: Could you answer the following question? And any insights would be great!

#HR #humanresourcesprofessional #hrprofessional

(And yes I see my grammatical error - but you cannot edit the poll just the info in the post - good to know for the future!)

Are you currently experience burnout?
You can see how people vote. Learn more

*Note: within less than 5 minutes, I already had 2 "yes" answers on the survey! The survey will be up for HR professionals to answer for three days.

Jodi Brandstetter
Best Selling Author CEO & Entrepreneur Speaker Self-Publishing C...
2m · 👥

When you are in HR, one of your main goals is to help your employees have a good work environment which includes limiting burnout. Curious if HR is experiencing burnout, how can they help other employees?

Question to #hrprofessional #humanresourcesprofessional:
What does it feel like to be ensuring others are not experiencing burnout while experiencing burnout yourself?

#HR #humanresources

👍 Like   💬 Comment

*Note: If I do not get any feedback on this within a day, I will start to tag HR professionals in the post and send LinkedIn messages to HR professionals as well to help my reach and boost engagement.

Observation

The goal of the observation is to understand how HR professionals communicate concerns and their ability to open up about their concerns or needs. Also, I am looking at body language to see if they are being open or showing negativity through their body.

Here is my Who, Where, and What for this challenge:

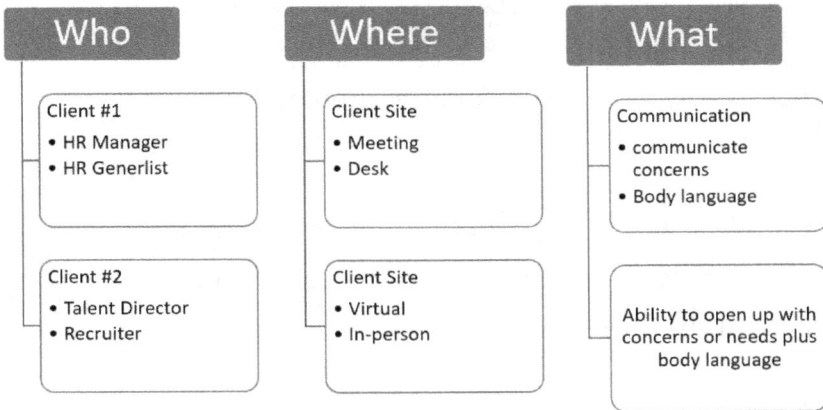

Who	Where	What
Client #1 • HR Manager • HR Generlist	**Client Site** • Meeting • Desk	**Communication** • communicate concerns • Body language
Client #2 • Talent Director • Recruiter	**Client Site** • Virtual • In-person	Ability to open up with concerns or needs plus body language

*Note: I will be shadowing both clients during the same week and will review my findings at the end of the week.

Interviewing

The goal of the interviews is to understand how HR professionals deal with burnout and if they believe dealing with their burnout can help them deal with other employees' burnout.

Here are my questions for the interview:

- Have you experienced burnout in your career? When and how? Do you know why?
- How did you help yourself during your feelings of burnout?
- Did your manager, team, or company help? If yes, what did they do?
- If someone said that they wanted to help you with burnout, what would you want?
- Have you been asked to help employees with burnout? If yes, how did you come up with a solution, and what is the solution?
- Did you think a solution for HR with burnout help other departments? Why?

My goal is to get at least 3 individuals to answer these questions. Here is my list of potential HR professionals to reach out to for the interview.

- Kate Legters, VP of HR
- Lynsey Gaca, Senior HR Business Partner
- Melanie Booher, Culture Coach
- Julia Pfirrman, Sr. Director, HR Business Partner

*Note: I will be reaching out and conducting these interviews the same week that I am observing my clients and asking questions via LinkedIn.

Gather Insights

Now that I have taken the time to understand my audience, it is time for me to review my notes and pull out my insights from the immersion of empathy, observation, and interviewing.

Here are my notes:

From Immersion in Empathy:

Jodi Brandstetter
Best Selling Author 🔲 CEO & Entrepreneur ✏️ Speaker 🔲 Self-Publishing C...
1w • Edited • 🌐

#HumanResources: Could you answer the following question? And any insights would be great!

#HR #humanresourcesprofessional #hrprofessional

(And yes I see my grammatical error - but you cannot edit the poll just the info in the post - good to know for the future!)

Are you currently experience burnout?
You can see how people vote. Learn more

Yes	56%
No	44%

80 votes • Poll closed

In the LinkedIn poll, 80 people answered the question and 56% said "yes" to currently experiencing burnout. The open-ended question that I added to LinkedIn did not receive any response. I decided to include this in the interview section.

Observation:

Client Site Meeting:

During the meeting, one HR professional stated that her cup was overflowing and needed others to help her with specific projects. Once others took on those items, the tension in her body lessened. Another HR professional needed to release stress by communicating issues or lack of information. Once he did this, the tension went away.

Client Site At the Desk:

While observing HR professionals at their desk, I noticed that there was a lot of notifications going on via their computer. One HR professional was trying to complete a task but kept getting pulled by an email notification, direct message, text message, and/or phone call. A task that should have taken minutes ended up taking about 15. His body language changed each time he had to do something outside of his intended task.

Virtual Meeting:

While conducting virtual training, an HR professional had to take two calls from candidates about offers. The urgency for these offers outweighed the training that was being presented. At the end of the training, he stated that he was swamped with work and was concerned he would not be able to handle the additional work I was asking of him. After providing some ideas on how to combine current work with the items I have requested plus mentioning that he can call or text me to help him, I could see the tension in his face melt away.

Interview:

I was able to interview four HR professionals about burnout.

Have you experienced burnout in your career? When and why?

- 3 out of 4 had experienced burnout in their career.
- One stated that she had burnout when her role was

only recruiting.

- One stated it was due to scheduling, not being fully trained, and a toxic workplace.
- One stated it was due to too many hours and not feeling appreciated.

How did you help yourself during burnout?

- One reached out to the manager and was able to add projects that helped her with having more of variety.
- One reached out to update her schedule and VP stated they do not do that.
- Two left the company to pursue a better work environment.

Did your manager, team, or company help? If yes, what did they do?

- One saw that her boss was also burnt out and did not ask for help.
- One was forward with her concerns; changes happened but unfortunately did not last long.

If someone said that they wanted to help you with burnout, what would you want?

- Just someone to talk to about the stress of the work.
- Ask for negative and toxic behaviors to be addressed.
- More focus on career path and development including ERGs, online courses, and cross-training

opportunities.
- Ensure time off is truly used to get some much-needed time away.
- Flexibility with hours (4-10 hour days or flexible on the start time or end time).
- No-meeting days.
- Recognition for a job well done.

Have you been asked to help employees with burnout? If yes, how did you come up with a solution, and what is the solution?

- Utilize engagement surveys to put together an action plan per department.
- Review staffing levels and remove any barriers to their success.
- For leaders with burnout, focus on the "why." Understand how their passion is now dulled, and remember why they decided to be a leader or entrepreneur.
- Focus on rediscovering the role and tie that to something meaningful.

Did you think a solution for HR with burnout help other departments? Why?

- If HR is burnt out, the company will reflect that.
- Yes, it will help and HR can be an example for other departments.
- Share learnings from HR with others and take the

opportunity to make things better for everyone.

Themes from Immersion in Empathy, Observation, and Interviewing:

I reviewed my notes and looked for themes. Here are the themes that I found:

HR professionals are or have been burnt out in their careers. The definition of "burnt-out" is different for people. Some will call it burnout, stress, less engagement, or simply not being happy. Understanding the person helps you understand their definition of burnt out.

The main theme is understanding the person and focusing the support on what the individual needs. Not everyone likes the same recognition. Not everyone wants a four-day-work-week. In order to help prevent burnout, understanding the person is the top priority.

HR can be an example of how to do this for a company. Starting with HR can impact the business, positively, and HR can provide the learnings to the business.

What do I want to explore through ideation?

The main question is how can you customize a program

for everyone? The solution needs to be flexible enough that each person can benefit from the solution.

Understanding your audience gives you the ability to ensure that you can move forward with ideation and your audience will be considered while building the solution. Now let's explore and take our insights to ideation.

Notes

1. https://conferences.shrm.org/conference/2019-annual-conference-exposition/session/employee-trauma-what-happened-vegas-didnt-stay
2. Kate Legters, Interviewee, Vice President of HR at Etergent [Interview]. 14 January 2022.

Observation Template:

Planning: Before observation, you must know **who** to observe, **where** to observe and **what** to look for.

Who	Where	What

Observation Notes:

Who:	
Where:	
Observations:	
Insights:	

Who:	
Where:	
Observations:	
Insights:	

Interviewing Template:

Based on your Challenge Statement, decide who you want to interview and select up to 10 questions that will help you learn about the challenge and audience.

Interview Questions:

Notes from Interviews:

Overall Insights:

Overall Themes:

Quotes:

Stories:

5.

Ideation

> "People are very open-minded about new things, as long as they're exactly like the old ones." –Charles F. Kettering [1]

I'm sure you probably have heard something like, "That's not how we do…" or "We have always done it this way." This is something a lot of people hear from HR! In general, it can be hard to change. However, change brings new ideas and different ways to do things. While interviewing a rock star HR professional and a dear friend of mine, Lynsey Gaca, for this book, she talked about how HR needs to be disrupters. Lynsey discussed the importance to HR being relevant, understanding the business, and being future forward-thinking.

During our conversation, I asked Lynsey about how she has been a disrupter. At first, Lynsey was thinking on a larger scope and could not think of one example. Once she started to think about being a disrupter in her company, she had several examples. A few examples are: getting her company to get away from paper and focus on electronic workflow, and re-vamping benefits to improve retention. She is always willing to provide her perspective, obtain the business, and employee's perspective to come up with different ideas to improve the business.

Lynsey stated, "HR needs time to creatively problem solve, come up with new ideas, and take time to disrupt their organization and our industry," Creative problem solving and coming up with ideas is the definition of ideation.[2]

Creativity and thinking outside the box gives you the ability to find a real solution that works for your audience *and* the business. Ideation is the design thinking tool that accomplishes this. I love ideation. I love post-it notes!

Now that I have a good understanding of my audience, I can take the time to come up with ideas that may help solve this challenge. There are four different ways to complete the ideation step.

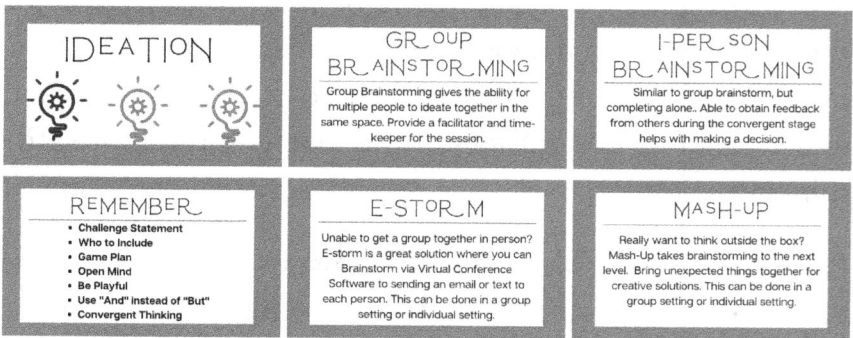

IDEATION

GROUP BRAINSTORMING
Group Brainstorming gives the ability for multiple people to ideate together in the same space. Provide a facilitator and time-keeper for the session.

1-PERSON BRAINSTORMING
Similar to group brainstorm, but completing alone.. Able to obtain feedback from others during the convergent stage helps with making a decision.

REMEMBER
- Challenge Statement
- Who to Include
- Game Plan
- Open Mind
- Be Playful
- Use "And" instead of "But"
- Convergent Thinking

E-STORM
Unable to get a group together in person? E-storm is a great solution where you can Brainstorm via Virtual Conference Software to sending an email or text to each person. This can be done in a group setting or individual setting.

MASH-UP
Really want to think outside the box? Mash-Up takes brainstorming to the next level. Bring unexpected things together for creative solutions. This can be done in a group setting or individual setting.

For this challenge, I will be using the Mash-Up Brainstorming and E-storming technique. I will be completing the brainstorming alone and asking others to provide feedback during the convergent stage.

Mash-Up

Challenge Statement: How might we take the burnout question and focus on finding a solution for the HR team that can be implemented for other departments in the company?

2 Different Categories: Therapy and Performance Review

I am going to brainstorm words or phrases that come to mind for both Therapy and Performance Review for two minutes.

Here is my list for Therapy and Performance Review:

THERAPY		PERFORMANCE REVIEW	
Physical	Therapist	Yearly	Short
Occupational	Questions	Boss	Not a lot of information
Mental	Answers	Feedback	Same each year
Psychology	Probing	Merit	Same as others
Coach	Uncomfortable	Grading	Communicate
Emotions	Learn About Yourself	Evaluation	Strengths
Family	Confidential	Positive	Concerns
Spouse	Guide	Negative	HR
Mom	Spiritual	Not sure what to say	System
Dad	Hard to Talk	Cheerleader	Generic questions
Problems	Open	Advocate	Specific to role
Talk	Communicate	Upset	Metrics
In-person	Monthly	Happy	KPIs
Virtual	Set Time	Accomplishments	Values
Private	Consistent		

Looking at my list for therapy, I started to focus on the

different types of therapy and immediately focused on psychotherapy. For performance reviews, I focus mostly on what happens during the performance review meeting including emotions and expectations.

Now, I select one item from each list and brainstorm for 15 minutes how to combine the two items together to solve the challenge statement. I have decided to select "Learn About Yourself" and "Specific to the Role."

My question is how can I mash "Learn About Yourself" and "Specific to the Role" to solve: How might we take the burnout question and focus on finding a solution for the HR team that can be implemented for other departments in the company?

Here are my ideas:

Therapy: Learn About Yourself AND Performance Review: Specific to the Role

Take the time throughout the year to understand you as a person and how that impacts your role. Have a consistent time to evaluate the role, time, personal life, and how that impacts your mental health. Maybe an app that triggers a review that includes not all your job but your mindset.

Idea 1: An app that pushes survey questions at different times of the year (monthly, quarterly, bi-yearly, and yearly) that asks about work and mindset. This is provided to the leader to understand how workload is impacting mental health of employees.

When you come to work, you become a worker and your personal life can be pushed to the side. How can a manager get to know their employee and be able to build a relationship where an employee will let them know when they are starting to feel burnout or stress? Is there a way to facilitate a "get to know you" meeting between employee and manager, or team and manager, where discussion around how you handle a high load of work, stress, or burnout? Encourage managers to dig deeper with employees on this. Is there an assessment that helps employees and managers see the triggers or the side effects of burnout based on the person?

Idea 2: An assessment that provides a better understanding of a person's triggers and side effects of stress and burnout. Manager and team receive this information so that they can keep an eye on potential burnout and work with employees or let a manager know.

Are there specific times in the year when stress can have a bigger impact? How can leaders help with this? In HR there are specific deadlines that can cause extra work or extra time devoted to a specific task. How can this be resolved, or how can managers understand when a person's cup is overflowing? Is there an app or text that can be sent where employees show their stress level – similar to the pain scale at hospitals and managers are notified when it gets too high or a meeting is immediately scheduled for manager and employee to meet?

Idea 3: A text OR email that asks, on a scale of 1-10, where is your stress level, and based on the number, a meeting is arranged with a manager or mental health coach. Training will be needed for the manager to make this a good meeting with resources. Or the employee can select their preference between manager and mental health coach before the meeting is scheduled.

Taking the time to talk about mental health and provide real examples of individuals in the company who have experienced burnout. Burnout can feel isolating and like you should not tell someone about it. There are often negative thoughts about being open about this. Provide an environment where discussing mental health is normal and common. Ask employees to speak and create a space where others can listen without judgment.

Idea 4: Establish a fireside chat with employees who have felt burnout and allow others to listen to their stories. Ideally, start with leadership or HR to tell their story. Ensure it is a safe place to provide this information.

From here, I need to focus on converging and focus on what ideas I want to consider executing.

Here are the ideas I have selected.

Idea 3: A text OR email that asks on a scale of 1-10, where is your stress level, and based on the number, a meeting is arranged with the manager or mental health coach. Training will be needed for the manager to make this a good meeting with resources. Or the employee can select their preference between manager and mental health coach before the meeting is scheduled. **Idea 4:** Establish a fireside chat with employees who have felt burnout and allow others to listen to their stories. Ideally, start with leadership or HR to tell their story. Ensure it is a safe place to provide this information. Now I am going to use E-storming to ensure that I have some ideas from others to be included in my list to converge.

E-storming

For e-storming, I am going to send an email to my ideal audience and ask them to provide 1-2 ideas to solve the challenge statement. The goal is to obtain an additional 10-20 ideas to review.

Here is the email:

Subject Line: E-storm Sprint – Burnout – Today Only!

Hi All!

Wanted to reach out to my fellow HR innovators for a quick 3-minute E-STORM Challenge!

<u>The Challenge</u>: How might we take the burnout question and focus on finding a solution for the HR team that can

be implemented for other departments in the company? Looking for any and all ideas on ways to solve burnout in HR.

<u>Idea Examples:</u> Ensure leaders have talking points to ask employees about mental health during one-on-one meetings, an app that helps employees with different ways to lower stress, "Get Out of Work" Card when life gets to be too much

<u>Ask</u>: Take a few minutes to reply to this email by EOD with 1 to 2 ideas.

<u>What do I get in return:</u>

Lots of ideas from HR professionals on burnout!

Your idea could be featured in my new book, *HR By Design*.

A virtual High Five, Fist Bump, or Hug from me!

A potential solution to provide to individuals who are suffering burnout at work!

Thank you so much! I am excited to see and hear your ideas!

Ideas from E-storm

By the end of the day, I received the following ideas:

Idea 1: Schedule "Lunch and Learns" that cover stress

management and burnout by having health professionals act as guest speakers to provide expert knowledge on the effects of stress. Helping employees deal with stress effectively will help them take care of their bodies and limit the physical and mental damages that stress can cause.

Idea 2: Offering a flexible schedule that includes working from home when needed and flexible hours can eliminate a lot of the daily workplace stress employees face. HR professionals will feel like they have more control over their own schedule and work environment, which will increase morale and reduce the chances of work overload.

Idea 3: Start and end each one-on-one with your team with, "How can I help you?" This gives the employee the ability to provide what they need to get their job done and lets them know that the manager cares about them.

Idea 4: Limit the number of meetings or a time limit on meetings. HR professionals have a lot of different responsibilities and when they are always in meetings, they cannot get their job done. Create a meeting survey to ensure that the meeting is truly needed and could not be accomplished or addressed with an email or phone call. Require time between meetings so that individuals are not going from one meeting to another, back-to-back.

Idea 5: "Get Out of Work" Card is provided to each member on the team to be used when they need a mental health day. Once someone uses it, give them another one. Ensure that this is actually something the team can use when they need it.

Here are the ideas I have selected from the e-storm.

Idea 3: Start and end each one-on-one with your team with, "How can I help you?" This gives the employee the ability to provide what they need to get their job done and lets them know that the manager cares about them.

Idea 5: "Get Out of Work" Card is provided to each member of the team to be used when they need a mental health day. Once someone uses it, give them another one. Ensure that this is actually something the team can use when they need it.

Convergent Thinking

Now that I have a list of ideas on how to solve the challenge, I need to use convergent thinking to select the idea I want to move to the prototype stage.

First I took the ideas and put them into similarity clusters:

The main cluster is: focus on the person and his or her needs. Each idea provides a way to understand the person and provides different ways to lower burnout.

Then, I made my final decision on what idea I will move to the prototyping step.

My final idea is a mashup of the ideas. It is an app that provides different ways to help the employee with recognizing burnout and finding ways to lower or eliminate burnout. The app will have features where:

- Text or Email can be sent to gauge burnout on a scale of 1-8 and based on the level, additional support will be provided in a variety of ways.
- Virtual Fire Side chats with employees as well as experts on burnout.
- Reminders to leadership on how to engage employees to understand their workload and provide assistance.
- Reminders on vacation time not being used or resources not being used based on the employee.
- Data and Reports to help leaders see how employees are handling burnout and success stories provided by employees, management, or HR.

By taking the time to complete two ideation methods, I had several ideas to consider. The ideas connected to each other and gave me the ability to mash the ideas up into one big idea. I also enjoyed connecting with other HR professionals and combining their ideas with mine. Overall, I found using two ideation methods to be a success for this challenge.

One of my favorite quotes which I included in my first book is by Nolan Bushnell:

"Everyone who's ever taken a shower has an idea. It's the person who gets out of the shower, dries off and does something about it who makes a difference."

I am now going to be the person who gets out of the shower, dries off, and creates a prototype with this idea.

Notes

1. https://www.thebalancesmb.com/funny-change-quotes-2892521
2. Lynsey Gaca, Interviewee, Sr. HR Business Partner at Ascendum Solutions [Interview]. 18 January 2022.

Brainstorming Facilitation Information:

Brainstorming is a creative strategy for teams to generate ideas when they are trying to come up with quick potential solutions to a challenge.

- Set Up:
  - Use your Challenge Statement for the brainstorming session
  - Space with no distractions (conference room, off site meeting space, etc.)
  - Designated Timekeeper and Facilitator
  - Materials: post-it notes, markers, and a blank wall for recording ideas
  - Decide on Individual or Group Brainstorming (5-6 people in group)
  - Decide on the number of minutes to brainstorm (10-15 minutes).
- Rules:
  - Defer judgment
  - Generate as many ideas as possible – the good, the bad, and the ugly.
  - Stay focused on the challenge statement
  - After brainstorming, the group will bucket ideas by themes, discuss ideas and vote for their favorite(s).
- During the brainstorm session:
  - Gather ideas and count the number of ideas
  - Bucket Ideas in Themes
  - Vote on Ideas
  - Select Idea to move forward to prototyping

6.

Prototype

While completing my research for this book, I spoke to Robin Throckmorton, President of strategic HR inc, an HR outsourcing company located in Cincinnati, OH. In our conversation, we chatted about design thinking and I asked her if she had used design thinking before in her role. Robin said "yes" and we ventured forward in the different ways she has used design thinking including observation, interviewing, and prototyping. But she used a different word for prototyping. Robin used "pilot." She discussed that when creating pieces of training for her clients, she will create a pilot course. The pilot course gives her the ability to test out the course, get feedback, and tweak the course if needed before implementing it.

In HR, we use all kinds of prototypes from pilots, to drafts, to sandboxes. The main goal of all of these is to test out the potential solution, get feedback, and ensure the solution works for the person and the business.

It is now time to take the selected idea and create the prototype. Remember, the prototype needs to be quick to create, cheap, and give the ability to test it out. There are all kinds of ways to create a prototype. Here are a few ways:

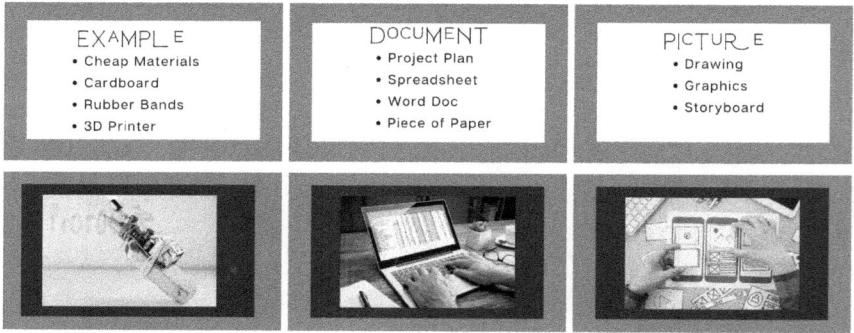

EXAMPLE	DOCUMENT	PICTURE
• Cheap Materials	• Project Plan	• Drawing
• Cardboard	• Spreadsheet	• Graphics
• Rubber Bands	• Word Doc	• Storyboard
• 3D Printer	• Piece of Paper	

Prototype

Here is the idea that was selected to move forward to become a prototype:

It is an app that provides different ways to help the employee with recognizing burnout and finding ways to lower or eliminate burnout.

The app will have features where:

- Text or Email can be sent to gauge burnout on a scale of 1-10 and based on the level, additional support will be provided in a variety of ways.
- Virtual Fire Side chats with employees as well as experts on burnout.
- Reminders to leadership on how to engage employees to understand their workload and provide assistance.
- Reminders on vacation time not being used or

resources not being used based on the employee.

- Data and Reports to help leaders see how employees are handling burnout and success stories provided by employees, management, or HR.

I have decided to use a graphic with content on how to use the app to transform the idea into a prototype.

TRIPLE R EFFECT

GO FROM BURNOUT TO REFRESH, REJUVENATE AND REVITALIZE

SCREEN ONE	SCREEN TWO	SCREEN THREE	SCREEN FOUR

SCREEN ONE
Company Email
Password
Sign In

Utilize Company Single Sign On
Employee does not need a
New Username/Password
Easy for them to get on app

SCREEN TWO
Welcome!
We want to get to know your better.
First let's confirm a few items.
Next

App will be connected to
HRIS system and pull
employee's information.

SCREEN THREE
Is this correct?
Name: Joe Doe
Phone: 555.5555
Email: n@email.com
Title: VP, HR
Yes
No

Employee verifies name,
phone, email and title.
If incorrect, they can update
& HR receives update for records.

SCREEN FOUR
Hi Joe!
We have a few questions to help us get to know you better and ensure we provide you with the right tools.

Our goal is provide you resources to help with stress and burnout.
Next

The goal is to understand
what type of resources &
tools the employee wants
to use to help with burnout.

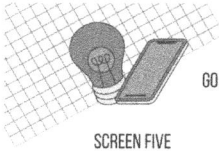

TRIPLE R EFFECT
GO FROM BURNOUT TO REFRESH, REJUVENATE AND REVITALIZE

SCREEN FIVE	SCREEN SIX	SCREEN SEVEN	SCREEN EIGHT

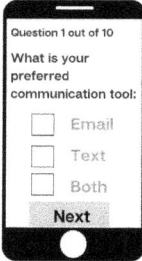

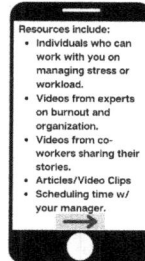

SCREEN FIVE

Question 1 out of 10

What is your preferred communication tool:

☐ Email
☐ Text
☐ Both

Next

Create questions that help tailor the information to the employee. Questions provided by expert in burnout.

SCREEN SIX

Thank you!

Now that we know you. Let's tell you a little bit about us!

Next

SCREEN SEVEN

Our goal is to help you with managing your workload and life!

We provide tools and resources via email and text.

Next

The goal is to provide resources that match what the employees wants or works best for them.

SCREEN EIGHT

Resources include:
• Individuals who can work with you on managing stress or workload.
• Videos from experts on burnout and organization.
• Videos from co-workers sharing their stories.
• Articles/Video Clips
• Scheduling time w/ your manager.

There is a repository of different tools including coaches, articles, videos and a way to connect manager..

TRIPLE R EFFECT
GO FROM BURNOUT TO REFRESH, REJUVENATE AND REVITALIZE

SCREEN NINE	SCREEN TEN	SCREEN ELEVEN	TEXT EXAMPLE

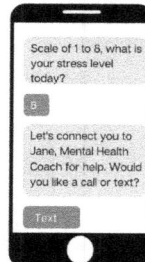

SCREEN NINE

The best part....
• The support is customized for you!
• We will use your preferred communication tool.
• We will use the information you provided to us to provide the right tools and resources for you!

Next

All content will be provided when and where the employee wants to receive it.

SCREEN TEN

Do you need to check in on this app?

NO!

You can use this app to update your survey so that we can customize your resources and tools moving forward.

Or we can update the survey via email/text.

Next

The app can be just to obtain the information and coordinate the communications. Or additional resources could be added to the app.

SCREEN ELEVEN

Thank you!

We are excited to help you be the best version of you!

TEXT EXAMPLE

Scale of 1 to 8, what is your stress level today?

8

Let's connect you to Jane, Mental Health Coach for help. Would you like a call or text?

Text

A text or email will be sent to employees on a scheduled time. Based on how employee answers will determine what and how we provide assistance.

TRIPLE R EFFECT
GO FROM BURNOUT TO REFRESH, REJUVENATE AND REVITALIZE

EMAIL EXAMPLE

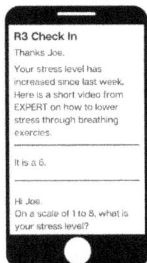

R3 Check In
Thanks Joe.
Your stress level has increased since last week. Here is a short video from EXPERT on how to lower stress through breathing exercises.

It is a 6.

Hi Joe.
On a scale of 1 to 8, what is your stress level?

A 7 or 8 level of stress will notify Mental Health Coach; 4 to 6 will notify the manager.

MANAGER NOTIFICATION

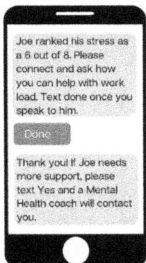

Joe ranked his stress as a 6 out of 8. Please connect and ask how you can help with work load. Text done once you speak to him.

Done

Thank you! If Joe needs more support, please text Yes and a Mental Health coach will contact you.

Notification to Manager can include how to handle the situation and assistance from HR or Mental Health Coach.

REPORTING

25% of employees responded to weekly stress level communication.

% of level of stress this month.

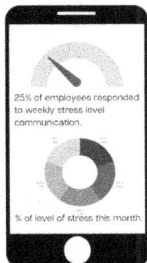

Reporting can be customized based on the area of business to manager to location, etc.

SUCCESS STORIES

Success stories will be given to HR to share with team or approved to be pushed to employees.

Now that I have my prototype, I need to share the prototype and obtain feedback from the audience and stakeholders. I have decided to share the prototype with the following people:

- Kate Legters, VP of HR
- Lynsey Gaca, Senior HR Business Partner
- Melanie Booher, Culture Coach
- Julia Pfirrman, Sr. Director, HR Business Partner
- Mary Johnson, Employee Development Manager

Feedback on Prototype

I received feedback from 2 individuals on the prototype.

One individual's concerns were around if the person in burnout knows how to answer the questions via the app and who would be the best person for that individual to talk to when they need someone? Would it be a mental health professional or someone within the company? She also stated that having resources to help with coping skills or resiliency would be beneficial. And that this type of app would be beneficial for industries with high stress.

The other individual provided me with the overall look and feel of the app and clarity on the 1-8 scale. She also provided me with feedback on the logo of the app. The background felt "hyper-speed" and the app should have a more calming effect. She also stated that having the app integrated into HRIS and wellness vendor's tools would be a huge benefit for HR. And if the app can help with lowering benefit costs and make it easier for the employees to use, those are big benefits too.

Insights from Feedback and Reflection

After creating the app, I was curious if it even needed to be an app. Could the solution be easier? Based on the feedback, what I created was more of like a check-in with employees and a connector to resources. Since individuals have different definitions of burnout, I need to find a question that can help address burnout without saying "burnout" to be more inclusive and over-arching. Gauging stress levels, and providing individuals the ability to choose what is best for them, will make this easier for both the individual and the company.

Based on the feedback and insights, I need to create text/ email software that integrates with key software systems like HRIS and Wellness Software. The software asks one question: "On a scale of 1 to 8, 1 being low and 8 being high, what is your stress level today?" Based on the employee's answer, the software will provide options for them to select. This data is stored in the HRIS system so that HR can use it to gauge overall stress in the company.

Here is the final prototype:

TRIPLE R EFFECT

GO FROM BURNOUT TO REFRESH, REJUVENATE AND REVITALIZE

TEXT EXAMPLE

Hi Joe. Its R3, your wellness connector. Wanted to check in and see how you are doing. Are you available chat by text?

Yes

Scale of 1 to 8, 1 being low and 8 being high what is your stress level today?

8

Sounds like you are under a lot of stress. We want to connect you with someone who can help you.

Would you like to talk to:
1. Your Manager
2. Your HR Rep
3. Wellness Coach
4. Someone Else
Type the # you prefer.

2

We will reach out to your HR Rep, NAME, to contact you via phone. Should s/he call you at this number?

Yes

Ok. We will reach out tomorrow to see how you are doing.

Hi Joe. How did your conversation with NAME go yesterday?

It went well.

Good. Your HR Rep wanted us to provide you with these resources. Click Here

If you need any additional assistance, just text back.

The Text Software is connected to the HRIS system and pulls phone number to text the employee. The goal is to gauge stress level and provide assistance.

Based on the employee's ranking of stress, R3 will provide up to 3 potential resources including people to talk to. Employee chooses.

HRIS will have HR Rep connected to employees so that R3 can direct any updates/concerns directly to HR. HR can provide to manager or wellness vendor.

R3 always reaches out the following day to re-connect with employee and provide any additional assistance necessary.

TRIPLE R EFFECT

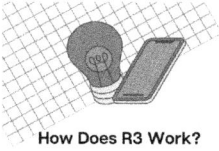

GO FROM BURNOUT TO REFRESH, REJUVENATE AND REVITALIZE

R3

How Does R3 Work?

R3 connects to your HRIS system and retrieves employee's email and cell phone number. R3 connects with employee (weekly/bi-weekly/monthly - up to employer) and asks on a scale of 1 to 8, 1 being low and 8 being high, what is your stress level? Based on the employee's answer, R3 provides 3 options to assist the employee with his/her stress level. Employee can select an option. R3 will follow up the next day to see how the employee is doing and if s/he needs additional assistance. Stress level and options selected will be housed in the HRIS and available for reporting.

R3 can provide updates on activity as well as progress based on information provided by employees. With machine learning, R3 can adapt and provide different options based on historical information. The goal is to understand the employee and the best solutions for stress management.

Benefits of R3

- Simple Check In Text/Email to gauge employee's stress level and provide the right resources.
- Able to connect via text and email.
- Integrates with HRIS, Benefit and Wellness vendor systems
  - Connects employees to the right people and resources including management, Human Resources, Wellness Vendors, EAP, Mental Health Coach, etc.
- Add On Benefit to current Benefit and Wellness programs
- Gauge Company Stress Level in real time
- Lower stress levels and lower benefit costs

The prototype is not the final solution. The final solution still needs to be created and pitched to key stakeholders. It is now time for iteration.

7.

Iteration

A lot of HR professionals have been in crisis management mode. With the Covid-19 pandemic, businesses have had uncertainty with sales, performance, and retaining employees plus different potential government mandates and the health and safety of their employees. A word used a lot has been "pivot." Now I would prefer to remember the word pivot from the T.V. show,*Friends*, versus a global pandemic. But the world *had* to pivot to keep moving forward. Another word for pivot is iteration.

Each time a company or a person had to change how they did something can be defined as iteration. And there has been a lot of iteration in the HR industry since 2020. HR is still in iterations with the great resignation and the future of work.

I prefer to be in iteration because I know staying in the same spot and not evolving does not help me grow and it will not help any company or industry grow. Throughout history, Human Resources as an industry has evolved. Let's look at the evolution of human resources.

An article on *ita group* reviews HR from pre-1900,

1920-1950, 1960-1980, and 1990-2010. Reviewing this article provided a nice overview of the evolution of HR and the key motivators for the changes.

In pre-1900, employees were expendable and productivity was the main focus. American companies realized that the employee's well-being correlated to productivity and companies started to focus on maintaining employees. In the 1920s-1950s, Personnel Departments and Labor Unions focused on training and compensation so that employees would stay longer and add more value to the companies. From the 1960s to the 1980s, the legislature passed around employment practices including the Equal Pay Act of 1963 and Civil Rights of 1964. And companies started to utilize industrial psychology with their selection of talent. From the time it was the 1990s to the 2010s, technology started to emerge and helped with administrative tasks and HR professionals could be more focused on employee engagement. From the 2010s to the present, technology is now being considered to assist with more than administrative tasks' employees are looking for meaningful work that gives them space to focus on themselves and their families and businesses are competing globally.[1]

Each change has focused on the employee and the business. Moving forward, HR will continue to iterate and focus on how to utilize technology and data to understand the business and employees, maintain a growth mindset to stay proactive in workforce planning, and be open to change when change comes because it will come. All of this is iteration.

Iteration includes more than just pivoting. It includes the ability to pitch the solution to the challenge, implement the solution and continue to test and gather feedback on the solution. A solution is not a solution until the key stakeholders approve the solution. And a solution is not a solution until it is implemented and used to solve the challenge. Just because a solution works today, it may not work in the future. Being able to test, gather feedback, and enhance or improve the solution will keep it a solution.

Let's look at the potential solution for our HR challenge and see how it can be pitched, implemented, used, and improved.

TRIPLE R EFFECT
GO FROM BURNOUT TO REFRESH, REJUVENATE AND REVITALIZE

TEXT EXAMPLE

Hi Joe. Its R3, your wellness connector. Wanted to check in and see how you are doing. Are you available chat by text?

Yes

Scale of 1 to 8, 1 being low and 8 being high what is your stress level today?

8

Sounds like you are under a lot of stress. We want to connect you with someone who can help you.

Would you like to talk to:
1. Your Manager
2. Your HR Rep
3. Wellness Coach
4. Someone Else
Type the # you prefer.

2

We will reach out to your HR Rep, NAME, to contact you via phone. Should s/he call you at this number?

Yes

Ok. We will reach out tomorrow to see how you are doing.

Hi Joe. How did your conversation with NAME go yesterday?

It went well.

Good. Your HR Rep wanted us to provide you with these resources. Click Here

If you need any additional assistance, just text back.

The Text Software is connected to the HRIS system and pulls phone number to text the employee. The goal is to gauge stress level and provide assistance.

Based on the employee's ranking of stress, R3 will provide up to 3 potential resources including people to talk to. Employee chooses.

HRIS will have HR Rep connected to employees so that R3 can direct any updates/concerns directly to HR. HR can provide to manager or wellness vendor.

R3 always reaches out the following day to re-connect with employee and provide any additional assistance necessary.

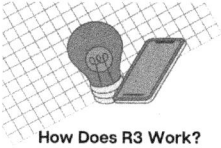

How Does R3 Work?

R3 connects to your HRIS system and retrieves employee's email and cell phone number. R3 connects with employee (weekly/bi-weekly/monthly - up to employer) and asks on a scale of 1 to 8, 1 being low and 8 being high, what is your stress level? Based on the employee's answer, R3 provides 3 options to assist the employee with his/her stress level. Employee can select an option. R3 will follow up the next day to see how the employee is doing and if s/he needs additional assistance. Stress level and options selected will be housed in the HRIS and available for reporting.

R3 can provide updates on activity as well as progress based on information provided by employees. With machine learning, R3 can adapt and provide different options based on historical information. The goal is to understand the employee and the best solutions for stress management.

Benefits of R3

- Simple Check In Text/Email to gauge employee's stress level and provide the right resources.
- Able to connect via text and email.
- Integrates with HRIS, Benefit and Wellness vendor systems
  - Connects employees to the right people and resources including management, Human Resources, Wellness Vendors, EAP, Mental Health Coach, etc.
- Add On Benefit to current Benefit and Wellness programs
- Gauge Company Stress Level in real time
- Lower stress levels and lower benefit costs

How To Pitch

There are several ways to pitch a solution. The pitch needs to focus on the key stakeholders and provide information to help them make a decision on the potential solution. For this solution, I will use these pitch methods:

- Storytelling
- Presentation with prototype

Storytelling Pitch

Set the stage:

"What a day! It's 2 p.m. and I still have not gotten anything off of my to-do list, I have to leave by 3:30 p.m. to get to my daughter's basketball game, and I have no clue what dinner looks like." *Ring Ring* "Hi. This is Jodi. What happened? The hiring manager has not greeted the candidate yet? The candidate got here 20 minutes ago! Ok. I will greet the candidate and get him into a conference room while you look for the manager."

While walking to greet the candidate, Jodi's phone buzzes. She looks down at the phone and it is a text from R3, the wellness connector asking her what level of her stress is today. Jodi texts a 7 out of 8. Based on Jodi's past stress level, this is much higher than usual. R3 texts and asks if Jodi wants to talk to someone or needs something else? Jodi texts back that she needs to focus on her tasks so she can get home for her daughter's basketball game. R3 texts Jodi's manager and lets her know that Jodi's stress level is high and needs help with work so she can leave at 3:30 p.m. Jodi's manager knows that Tuesday nights are Lena's, her daughter's, basketball night and wants to help Jodi out.

When Jodi gets back to her desk, there is a note from her manager. The note says, "Jodi. I am here for you. What can

I do to help you get to your daughter's game on time?"Jodi takes a deep breath and looks for her manager. Jodi's eyes meet her manager's eyes and both smile. Jodi's manager comes to her desk and says, "How can I help?" Just that question makes Jodi feel better and she is able to delegate a few items to her manager and peer, get the rest of her to-do list accomplished, and make it to her daughter's basketball game.

Presentation Pitch

I want to introduce R3, the wellness connector. R3 checks in with employees to understand their stress levels and provide ways to assist the employee. It's as easy as a text or email to find the level of stress and asking what can help you right now lower your stress levels. This can be a conversation with HR, a nudge to a manager to help out, a 2-minute meditation, or a quick video on how to say no when you need to say no.

R3 also helps the company by providing data on employees' stress levels and connecting this information to the company's HRIS system, benefit vendor, and wellness vendor. By using R3, your benefit-cost will go down on average by 15% and personal satisfaction goes up by 17%.

You have everything you need to help your employees with stress and burnout. It all starts with a text.

R3 is a fake company and the data above is not real.

By using the storytelling and presentation pitch methods, I was able to paint the picture of how this solution could benefit both the employee and the business. A solid pitch that hits both the mind and heart is important. The mind is all about the data and the heart is all about the person. Blending the two helps the key stakeholders see the impact of the solution for both the business and the employees.

How To Implement

Once you have the buy-in on your solution, it is time to implement it. This can be as simple as updating a policy or process. Or this can be a large project like implementing new software. By using design thinking, implementation can be very simplistic because all of the key stakeholders have bought into the new solution and are ready to move forward. It is now about putting the project plan together and executing it.

Feedback is still critical in the implementation phase. During implementation, learnings will come up that may move the solution in a different direction. And this is okay. Be open and willing to change directions when needed. The solution is not stagnant.

With the R3 solution, the implementation may include

looking for other vendors who have a similar product. Compare the competitors with R3 and understand the pros and cons of each. Based upon your reviewing of all vendors, you then decide on the best tool for the organization. From there, the organization can test the product in the HR department and gather insights on how well the product performs. There may be enhancements or changes to the product before implementation to the rest of the company. Testing the product out with one department, versus all, gives the company time to enhance the product and push out the best product to the whole company.

Continuous Improvement

Once the solution is implemented, iteration does not stop. Companies change, people change and solutions will need to change with this. Continuing to gather feedback, review the solution, and be willing to update will help companies stay competitive.

Continuous improvement is not fun. In fact, it can be downright annoying. Constant change feels hard. But continuous improvement is where solutions continue to be the solution needed.

Throughout my career, I have always said that the only thing constant is change. The goal is to make that change mean something to the people who are within the change. If the change is for the better, then the change has done its job.

Notes

1. https://www.itagroup.com/insights/evolution-of-human-resources-management

Conclusion

Congratulations! You now have a good understanding of what design thinking is and how it can be the methodology of choice for HR. The goal of this book was to provide the foundation of design thinking and show how design thinking can be implemented in your day-to-day within human resources. I hope this inspired and helped you to look at challenges in a different way while also seeing that HR can be the leader in change and that change can start in HR.

There was a reason why I chose burnout as the challenge for this book. Throughout my HR career, I have seen HR professionals either get close to burnout or fall victim to burnout. I think a reason HR can get to the level of burnout is that HR focuses on *others*. It can be hard for HR to focus on themselves. The main goal of HR is to support the company and the people. And HR does not see themselves as part of the people that they support in their role.

Having taken the time to look at HR burnout through design thinking, I hope you realized that focusing on you is critical to the success of your HR team, your employees, your organization, and YOU! Your health and your mindset need to be your priority so that you can help others. I love the analogy of filling your cup before you fill others' cups. We must take care of our minds and bodies to be assets to our teams, businesses, and families.

Filling my cup first has always been difficult for me to do. I now look at filling my cup in a different way. Once my cup is full and starts to overflow, that is when I can help others. I give them what is overflowing while I keep my cup full. By doing this, I am in the right mental state to share my passion and purpose with others.

Fill your cup and *then* you can use the overflow for others. Be willing to get outside your box and be creative with ways to help you and the people you support.

This book got me out of my box. When I was writing my first book, I believed that a book must have at least 30,000 words to be a solid informative book. It took me over 6 months to write, publish, and launch my first book. It was a lot of work, a lot of hours, and by the time it was published, I was drained. And I still had to market the book, create presentations around my book, and I had a goal of creating a course to go with the book. The book got published, marketing happened, and presentations were presented. But no course was created until now. It took me over a year to finally get the curriculum together.

While creating my curriculum for *Hire By Design*, I had a couple of "ah-ha" moments. My first "ah-ha" moment was that I wanted to create a course for HR professionals on how to use design thinking. My second "ah-ha" moment was that I needed a book to go with the design thinking course for HR. My third "ah-ha" moment was that I could write my book in a way that helps me build my course curriculum and presentation at the same time. My final "ah-ha" moment came in a meeting with one of my clients. My client believes that people want quick and simple pieces of training. He kept saying "micro-trainings." It was then that it dawned on me. I realized that this book could be a *micro*-book. My definition of a micro-book is less than 20,000 words and less than 100 pages.

Writing this book has been a test to see if I can create a book, a course, *and* a presentation all in one. The book is completed, the curriculum is set, and the presentation is now branded. Now it is time to put all of it out in the world and see if others want to become design thinkers.

Thank you for taking the time to read HR By Design. If you see design thinking as the methodology to solve HR challenges and problems, I encourage you to check out my course, HR By Design on By Design Brainery. This course will give you the ability to take an HR challenge and work through design thinking to find a solution. At the end of the course, you will have the confidence to take design thinking back to your workplace and help solve problems or challenges your team or business is facing. To learn more about the HR By Design course, please go to https://Learn.ByDesignBrainery.com.

I'm going to end this book the same way I ended my first book. Growing up in the late '80s and '90s, there was one public service announcement that I have consistently gone back to. It is " The More You Know..."

The more you know about yourself, your team, and your business, the more you will grow and help others grow as well.

~Jodi

Acknowledgments:

Every book is created with a tribe. There is so much that goes into writing a book. And I have found a tribe who kicks butt when it comes to producing and publishing. I also have found a tribe who loves me and want to help me with all of my crazy ideas including writing books!

A Big Thank You To:

Melanie Booher
Alex Glossner
Kelsey Grome

Lynsey Gaca
Kate Legters
Julie Pfirrman
Mary Johnson
Robin Throckmorton

Ron Brandstetter
Lena Brandstetter
Larry & Becky Harmeyer
Vanessa Wolf

About the Author:

Jodi Brandstetter

Jodi believes everyone can be a creative problem solver. It just takes the right method to make this happen. And design thinking is that method.

Jodi has 20 years of HR and recruiting experience, and is certified in design thinking. Her expertise in design thinking is a game changer for Human Resources and Talent Acquisition industries.

Jodi is the CEO of:

Lean Effective Talent Strategies - a talent acquisition consulting firm

Talent Acquisition Evolution - a community for recruiting professionals to connect, learn, and work together

Influence Network Media - a media company that provides production, publication and promotion services for business experts to write bestselling books.

Jodi lives outside of Cincinnati, OH with husband, Ron, daughter, Lena and her fur-children – Dali and Monet.

Connect with Jodi:
Email: Jodi@LETSCincy.com
LinkedIn: https://www.LinkedIn.com/in/jodibrandstetter

Also by Jodi Brandstetter

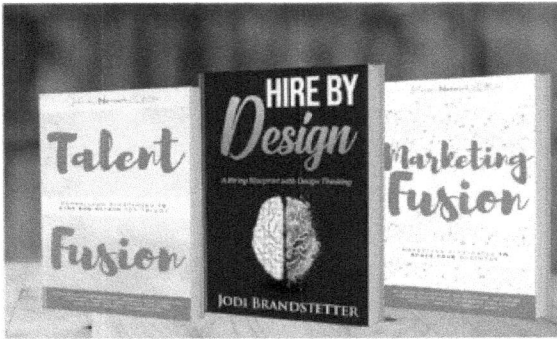

Talent Fusion, Compelling Strategies to Hire and Retain Top Talent

Hire By Design, A Hiring Blueprint with Design Thinking

Marketing Fusion, Marketing Strategies to Scale Your Business

Available on https://www.amazon.com/Jodi-Brandstetter/

About the Publisher:

Influence Network Media

We provide publishing & promotional services to business experts who want to become authors.

A media company that provides publishing and promotional coaching and services to authors who write non-fiction books around people in business. Founded by Jodi Brandstetter and Melanie Booher, Influence Network Media is a one-stop-shop to ensure your book is a bestseller and authors are able to use their book as a vessel to their career success.

Our offerings include:

- **Overnight Author** where in a day and a half you are an author of one of our collective book series.
- **Collective Book** Opportunities where you only need one chapter, bio and headshot to become an Amazon Best Selling Author!
- **Micro Book** Opportunities for Business Consultants who want to write a book that becomes a course and presentation all in one.

To learn more:
https://authors.influencenetworkmedia.com
Publishing@LETSCincy.com